MY
INTERNET ADDRESSES
& PASSWORD LOGBOOK

P A S S W O R D   L O G

ACTIVINOTES

Activinotes

DAILY JOURNALS, PLANNERS, NOTEBOOKS AND OTHER BLANK BOOKS

Copyright 2016

Name: _____

Website Address: _____

ID/Username: _____

Password: _____

Notes: _____

_____

Name: _____

Website Address: _____

ID/Username: _____

Password: _____

Notes: _____

_____

Name: _____

Website Address: _____

ID/Username: _____

Password: _____

Notes: _____

_____

Name: _____

Website Address: _____

ID/Username: _____

Password: _____

Notes: _____

_____

Name: _____

Website Address: _____

ID/Username: _____

Password: _____

Notes: _____

_____

Name: _____

Website Address: _____

ID/Username: _____

Password: _____

Notes: _____

_____

Name: _____

Website Address: _____

ID/Username: _____

Password: _____

Notes: _____

_____

Name: _____

Website Address: _____

ID/Username: _____

Password: _____

Notes: _____

_____

Name: _____

Website Address: _____

ID/Username: _____

Password: _____

Notes: _____

_____

Name: _____

Website Address: _____

ID/Username: _____

Password: _____

Notes: _____

_____

Name: _____

Website Address: _____

ID/Username: _____

Password: _____

Notes: _____

_____

Name: _____

Website Address: _____

ID/Username: _____

Password: _____

Notes: _____

_____

Name: _____

Website Address: _____

ID/Username: _____

Password: _____

Notes: _____

_____

Name: _____

Website Address: _____

ID/Username: _____

Password: _____

Notes: _____

_____

Name: _____

Website Address: _____

ID/Username: _____

Password: _____

Notes: _____

_____

Name: _____

Website Address: _____

ID/Username: _____

Password: _____

Notes: _____

_____

Name: _____

Website Address: _____

ID/Username: _____

Password: _____

Notes: _____

_____

Name: _____

Website Address: _____

ID/Username: _____

Password: _____

Notes: _____

_____

Name: _____

Website Address: _____

ID/Username: _____

Password: _____

Notes: _____

_____

Name: _____

Website Address: _____

ID/Username: _____

Password: _____

Notes: _____

_____

Name: _____

Website Address: _____

ID/Username: _____

Password: _____

Notes: _____

_____

Name: _____

Website Address: _____

ID/Username: _____

Password: _____

Notes: _____

_____

Name: _____

Website Address: _____

ID/Username: _____

Password: _____

Notes: _____

_____

Name: _____

Website Address: _____

ID/Username: _____

Password: _____

Notes: _____

_____

Name: _____

Website Address: _____

ID/Username: _____

Password: _____

Notes: _____

_____

Name: _____

Website Address: _____

ID/Username: _____

Password: _____

Notes: _____

_____

Name: _____

Website Address: _____

ID/Username: _____

Password: _____

Notes: _____

_____

Name: _____

Website Address: _____

ID/Username: _____

Password: _____

Notes: _____

_____

Name: _____

Website Address: _____

ID/Username: _____

Password: _____

Notes: _____

_____

Name: _____

Website Address: _____

ID/Username: _____

Password: _____

Notes: _____

_____

Name: _____

Website Address: _____

ID/Username: _____

Password: _____

Notes: _____

_____

Name: _____

Website Address: _____

ID/Username: _____

Password: _____

Notes: _____

_____

Name: _____

Website Address: _____

ID/Username: _____

Password: _____

Notes: _____

_____

Name: _____

Website Address: _____

ID/Username: _____

Password: _____

Notes: _____

_____

Name: _____

Website Address: _____

ID/Username: _____

Password: _____

Notes: _____

_____

Name: _____

Website Address: _____

ID/Username: _____

Password: _____

Notes: _____

_____

Name: _____

Website Address: _____

ID/Username: _____

Password: _____

Notes: _____

_____

Name: _____

Website Address: _____

ID/Username: _____

Password: _____

Notes: _____

_____

Name: _____

Website Address: _____

ID/Username: _____

Password: _____

Notes: _____

_____

Name: _____

Website Address: _____

ID/Username: _____

Password: _____

Notes: _____

_____

Name: _____

Website Address: _____

ID/Username: _____

Password: _____

Notes: _____

_____

Name: _____

Website Address: _____

ID/Username: _____

Password: _____

Notes: _____

_____

Name: _____

Website Address: _____

ID/Username: _____

Password: _____

Notes: _____

_____

Name: _____

Website Address: _____

ID/Username: _____

Password: _____

Notes: _____

_____

Name: _____

Website Address: _____

ID/Username: _____

Password: _____

Notes: _____

_____

Name: _____

Website Address: _____

ID/Username: _____

Password: _____

Notes: _____

_____

Name: _____

Website Address: _____

ID/Username: _____

Password: _____

Notes: _____

_____

Name: _____

Website Address: _____

ID/Username: _____

Password: _____

Notes: _____

_____

Name: _____

Website Address: _____

ID/Username: _____

Password: _____

Notes: _____

_____

Name: _____

Website Address: _____

ID/Username: _____

Password: _____

Notes: _____

_____

Name: _____

Website Address: _____

ID/Username: _____

Password: _____

Notes: _____

_____

Name: _____

Website Address: _____

ID/Username: _____

Password: _____

Notes: _____

_____

Name: _____

Website Address: _____

ID/Username: _____

Password: _____

Notes: _____

_____

Name: _____

Website Address: _____

ID/Username: _____

Password: _____

Notes: _____

_____

Name: _____

Website Address: _____

ID/Username: _____

Password: _____

Notes: _____

_____

Name: _____

Website Address: _____

ID/Username: _____

Password: _____

Notes: _____

_____

Name: _____

Website Address: _____

ID/Username: _____

Password: _____

Notes: _____

_____

Name: _____

Website Address: _____

ID/Username: _____

Password: _____

Notes: _____

_____

Name: _____

Website Address: _____

ID/Username: _____

Password: _____

Notes: _____

_____

Name: _____

Website Address: _____

ID/Username: _____

Password: _____

Notes: _____

_____

Name: _____

Website Address: _____

ID/Username: _____

Password: _____

Notes: _____

_____

Name: _____

Website Address: _____

ID/Username: _____

Password: _____

Notes: _____

_____

Name: _____

Website Address: _____

ID/Username: _____

Password: _____

Notes: _____

_____

Name: _____

Website Address: _____

ID/Username: _____

Password: _____

Notes: _____

_____

Name: _____

Website Address: _____

ID/Username: _____

Password: _____

Notes: _____

_____

Name: _____

Website Address: _____

ID/Username: _____

Password: _____

Notes: _____

_____

Name: _____

Website Address: _____

ID/Username: _____

Password: _____

Notes: _____

_____

Name: _____

Website Address: _____

ID/Username: _____

Password: _____

Notes: _____

_____

Name: _____

Website Address: _____

ID/Username: _____

Password: _____

Notes: _____

_____

Name: _____

Website Address: _____

ID/Username: _____

Password: _____

Notes: _____

_____

Name: _____

Website Address: _____

ID/Username: _____

Password: _____

Notes: _____

_____

Name: _____

Website Address: _____

ID/Username: _____

Password: _____

Notes: _____

_____

Name: _____

Website Address: _____

ID/Username: _____

Password: _____

Notes: _____

_____

Name: _____

Website Address: _____

ID/Username: _____

Password: _____

Notes: _____

_____

Name: _____

Website Address: _____

ID/Username: _____

Password: _____

Notes: _____

_____

Name: _____

Website Address: _____

ID/Username: _____

Password: _____

Notes: _____

_____

Name: _____

Website Address: _____

ID/Username: _____

Password: _____

Notes: _____

_____

Name: _____

Website Address: _____

ID/Username: _____

Password: _____

Notes: _____

_____

Name: _____

Website Address: _____

ID/Username: _____

Password: _____

Notes: _____

_____

Name: _____

Website Address: _____

ID/Username: _____

Password: _____

Notes: _____

_____

Name: _____

Website Address: _____

ID/Username: _____

Password: _____

Notes: _____

_____

Name: _____

Website Address: _____

ID/Username: _____

Password: _____

Notes: _____

_____

Name: _____

Website Address: _____

ID/Username: _____

Password: _____

Notes: _____

_____

Name: _____

Website Address: _____

ID/Username: _____

Password: _____

Notes: _____

_____

Name: _____

Website Address: _____

ID/Username: _____

Password: _____

Notes: _____

_____

Name: _____

Website Address: _____

ID/Username: _____

Password: _____

Notes: _____

_____

Name: _____

Website Address: _____

ID/Username: _____

Password: _____

Notes: _____

_____

Name: _____

Website Address: _____

ID/Username: _____

Password: _____

Notes: _____

_____

Name: _____

Website Address: _____

ID/Username: _____

Password: _____

Notes: _____

_____

Name: _____

Website Address: _____

ID/Username: _____

Password: _____

Notes: _____

_____

Name: _____

Website Address: _____

ID/Username: _____

Password: _____

Notes: _____

_____

Name: _____

Website Address: _____

ID/Username: _____

Password: _____

Notes: _____

_____

Name: _____

Website Address: _____

ID/Username: _____

Password: _____

Notes: _____

_____

Name: _____

Website Address: _____

ID/Username: _____

Password: _____

Notes: _____

_____

Name: _____

Website Address: _____

ID/Username: _____

Password: _____

Notes: _____

_____

Name: _____

Website Address: _____

ID/Username: _____

Password: _____

Notes: _____

_____

Name: _____

Website Address: _____

ID/Username: _____

Password: _____

Notes: _____

_____

Name: _____

Website Address: _____

ID/Username: _____

Password: _____

Notes: _____

_____

Name: _____

Website Address: _____

ID/Username: _____

Password: _____

Notes: _____

_____

Name: _____

Website Address: _____

ID/Username: _____

Password: _____

Notes: _____

_____

Name: _____

Website Address: _____

ID/Username: _____

Password: _____

Notes: _____

_____

Name: _____

Website Address: _____

ID/Username: _____

Password: _____

Notes: _____

_____

Name: _____

Website Address: _____

ID/Username: _____

Password: _____

Notes: _____

_____

Name: _____

Website Address: _____

ID/Username: _____

Password: _____

Notes: _____

_____

Name: _____

Website Address: _____

ID/Username: _____

Password: _____

Notes: _____

_____

Name: _____

Website Address: _____

ID/Username: _____

Password: _____

Notes: _____

_____

Name: _____

Website Address: _____

ID/Username: _____

Password: _____

Notes: _____

_____

Name: _____

Website Address: _____

ID/Username: _____

Password: _____

Notes: _____

_____

Name: _____

Website Address: _____

ID/Username: _____

Password: _____

Notes: _____

_____

Name: _____

Website Address: _____

ID/Username: _____

Password: _____

Notes: _____

_____

Name: _____

Website Address: _____

ID/Username: _____

Password: _____

Notes: _____

_____

Name: _____

Website Address: _____

ID/Username: _____

Password: _____

Notes: _____

_____

Name: _____

Website Address: _____

ID/Username: _____

Password: _____

Notes: _____

_____

Name: _____

Website Address: _____

ID/Username: _____

Password: _____

Notes: _____

_____

Name: _____

Website Address: _____

ID/Username: _____

Password: _____

Notes: _____

_____

Name: _____

Website Address: _____

ID/Username: _____

Password: _____

Notes: _____

_____

Name: _____

Website Address: _____

ID/Username: _____

Password: _____

Notes: _____

_____

Name: _____

Website Address: _____

ID/Username: _____

Password: _____

Notes: _____

_____

Name: _____

Website Address: _____

ID/Username: _____

Password: _____

Notes: _____

_____

Name: _____

Website Address: _____

ID/Username: _____

Password: _____

Notes: _____

_____

Name: _____

Website Address: _____

ID/Username: _____

Password: _____

Notes: _____

_____

Name: _____

Website Address: _____

ID/Username: _____

Password: _____

Notes: _____

_____

Name: _____

Website Address: _____

ID/Username: _____

Password: _____

Notes: _____

_____

Name: _____

Website Address: _____

ID/Username: _____

Password: _____

Notes: _____

_____

Name: _____

Website Address: _____

ID/Username: _____

Password: _____

Notes: _____

_____

Name: _____

Website Address: _____

ID/Username: _____

Password: _____

Notes: _____

_____

Name: _____

Website Address: _____

ID/Username: _____

Password: _____

Notes: _____

_____

Name: _____

Website Address: _____

ID/Username: _____

Password: _____

Notes: _____

_____

Name: _____

Website Address: _____

ID/Username: _____

Password: _____

Notes: _____

_____

Name: _____

Website Address: _____

ID/Username: _____

Password: _____

Notes: _____

_____

Name: _____

Website Address: _____

ID/Username: _____

Password: _____

Notes: _____

_____

Name: _____

Website Address: _____

ID/Username: _____

Password: _____

Notes: _____

_____

Name: _____

Website Address: _____

ID/Username: _____

Password: _____

Notes: _____

_____

Name: _____

Website Address: _____

ID/Username: _____

Password: _____

Notes: _____

_____

Name: _____

Website Address: _____

ID/Username: _____

Password: _____

Notes: _____

_____

Name: _____

Website Address: _____

ID/Username: _____

Password: _____

Notes: _____

_____

Name: _____

Website Address: _____

ID/Username: _____

Password: _____

Notes: _____

_____

Name: _____

Website Address: _____

ID/Username: _____

Password: _____

Notes: _____

_____

Name: _____

Website Address: _____

ID/Username: _____

Password: _____

Notes: _____

_____

Name: _____

Website Address: _____

ID/Username: _____

Password: _____

Notes: _____

_____

Name: _____

Website Address: _____

ID/Username: _____

Password: _____

Notes: _____

_____

Name: _____

Website Address: _____

ID/Username: _____

Password: _____

Notes: _____

_____

Name: _____

Website Address: _____

ID/Username: _____

Password: _____

Notes: _____

_____

Name: _____

Website Address: _____

ID/Username: _____

Password: _____

Notes: _____

_____

Name: _____

Website Address: _____

ID/Username: _____

Password: _____

Notes: _____

_____

Name: _____

Website Address: _____

ID/Username: _____

Password: _____

Notes: _____

_____

Name: _____

Website Address: _____

ID/Username: _____

Password: _____

Notes: _____

_____

Name: _____

Website Address: _____

ID/Username: _____

Password: _____

Notes: _____

_____

Name: _____

Website Address: _____

ID/Username: _____

Password: _____

Notes: _____

_____

Name: _____

Website Address: _____

ID/Username: _____

Password: _____

Notes: _____

_____

Name: _____

Website Address: _____

ID/Username: _____

Password: _____

Notes: _____

_____

Name: _____

Website Address: _____

ID/Username: _____

Password: _____

Notes: _____

_____

Name: _____

Website Address: _____

ID/Username: _____

Password: _____

Notes: _____

_____

Name: _____

Website Address: _____

ID/Username: _____

Password: _____

Notes: _____

_____

Name: _____

Website Address: _____

ID/Username: _____

Password: _____

Notes: _____

_____

Name: _____

Website Address: _____

ID/Username: _____

Password: _____

Notes: _____

_____

Name: _____

Website Address: _____

ID/Username: _____

Password: _____

Notes: _____

_____

Name: _____

Website Address: _____

ID/Username: _____

Password: _____

Notes: _____

_____

Name: _____

Website Address: _____

ID/Username: _____

Password: _____

Notes: _____

_____

Name: _____

Website Address: _____

ID/Username: _____

Password: _____

Notes: _____

_____

Name: _____

Website Address: _____

ID/Username: _____

Password: _____

Notes: _____

_____

Name: _____

Website Address: _____

ID/Username: _____

Password: _____

Notes: _____

_____

Name: _____

Website Address: _____

ID/Username: _____

Password: _____

Notes: _____

_____

Name: _____

Website Address: _____

ID/Username: _____

Password: _____

Notes: _____

_____

Name: _____

Website Address: _____

ID/Username: _____

Password: _____

Notes: _____

_____

Name: _____

Website Address: _____

ID/Username: _____

Password: _____

Notes: _____

_____

Name: _____

Website Address: _____

ID/Username: _____

Password: _____

Notes: _____

_____

Name: _____

Website Address: _____

ID/Username: _____

Password: _____

Notes: _____

_____

Name: _____

Website Address: _____

ID/Username: _____

Password: _____

Notes: _____

_____

Name: _____

Website Address: _____

ID/Username: _____

Password: _____

Notes: _____

_____

Name: _____

Website Address: _____

ID/Username: _____

Password: _____

Notes: _____

_____

Name: _____

Website Address: _____

ID/Username: _____

Password: _____

Notes: _____

_____

Name: _____

Website Address: _____

ID/Username: _____

Password: _____

Notes: _____

_____

Name: _____

Website Address: _____

ID/Username: _____

Password: _____

Notes: _____

_____

Name: _____

Website Address: _____

ID/Username: _____

Password: _____

Notes: _____

_____

Name: _____

Website Address: _____

ID/Username: _____

Password: _____

Notes: _____

_____

Name: _____

Website Address: _____

ID/Username: _____

Password: _____

Notes: _____

_____

Name: _____

Website Address: _____

ID/Username: _____

Password: _____

Notes: _____

_____

Name: _____

Website Address: _____

ID/Username: _____

Password: _____

Notes: _____

_____

Name: _____

Website Address: _____

ID/Username: _____

Password: _____

Notes: _____

_____

Name: _____

Website Address: _____

ID/Username: _____

Password: _____

Notes: _____

_____

Name: _____

Website Address: _____

ID/Username: _____

Password: _____

Notes: _____

_____

Name: _____

Website Address: _____

ID/Username: _____

Password: _____

Notes: _____

_____

Name: _____

Website Address: _____

ID/Username: _____

Password: _____

Notes: _____

_____

Name: _____

Website Address: _____

ID/Username: _____

Password: _____

Notes: _____

_____

Name: _____

Website Address: _____

ID/Username: _____

Password: _____

Notes: _____

_____

Name: _____

Website Address: _____

ID/Username: _____

Password: _____

Notes: _____

_____

Name: _____

Website Address: _____

ID/Username: _____

Password: _____

Notes: _____

_____

Name: _____

Website Address: _____

ID/Username: _____

Password: _____

Notes: _____

_____

Name: _____

Website Address: _____

ID/Username: _____

Password: _____

Notes: _____

_____

Name: _____

Website Address: _____

ID/Username: _____

Password: _____

Notes: _____

_____

Name: _____

Website Address: _____

ID/Username: _____

Password: _____

Notes: _____

_____

Name: _____

Website Address: _____

ID/Username: _____

Password: _____

Notes: _____

_____

Name: _____

Website Address: _____

ID/Username: _____

Password: _____

Notes: _____

_____

Name: _____

Website Address: _____

ID/Username: _____

Password: _____

Notes: _____

_____

Name: _____

Website Address: _____

ID/Username: _____

Password: _____

Notes: _____

_____

Name: _____

Website Address: _____

ID/Username: _____

Password: _____

Notes: _____

_____

Name: _____

Website Address: _____

ID/Username: _____

Password: _____

Notes: _____

_____

Name: _____

Website Address: _____

ID/Username: _____

Password: _____

Notes: _____

_____

Name: _____

Website Address: _____

ID/Username: _____

Password: _____

Notes: _____

_____

Name: _____

Website Address: _____

ID/Username: _____

Password: _____

Notes: _____

_____

Name: _____

Website Address: _____

ID/Username: _____

Password: _____

Notes: _____

_____

Name: _____

Website Address: _____

ID/Username: _____

Password: _____

Notes: _____

_____

Name: _____

Website Address: _____

ID/Username: _____

Password: _____

Notes: _____

_____

Name: _____

Website Address: _____

ID/Username: _____

Password: _____

Notes: _____

_____

Name: _____

Website Address: _____

ID/Username: _____

Password: _____

Notes: _____

_____

Name: _____

Website Address: _____

ID/Username: _____

Password: _____

Notes: _____

_____

Name: _____

Website Address: _____

ID/Username: _____

Password: _____

Notes: _____

_____

Name: _____

Website Address: _____

ID/Username: _____

Password: _____

Notes: _____

_____

Name: _____

Website Address: _____

ID/Username: _____

Password: _____

Notes: _____

_____

Name: _____

Website Address: _____

ID/Username: _____

Password: _____

Notes: _____

_____

Name: _____

Website Address: _____

ID/Username: _____

Password: _____

Notes: _____

_____

Name: _____

Website Address: _____

ID/Username: _____

Password: _____

Notes: _____

_____

Name: _____

Website Address: _____

ID/Username: _____

Password: _____

Notes: _____

_____

Name: _____

Website Address: _____

ID/Username: _____

Password: _____

Notes: _____

_____

Name: _____

Website Address: _____

ID/Username: _____

Password: _____

Notes: _____

_____

Name: _____

Website Address: _____

ID/Username: _____

Password: _____

Notes: _____

_____

Name: _____

Website Address: _____

ID/Username: _____

Password: _____

Notes: _____

_____

Name: _____

Website Address: _____

ID/Username: _____

Password: _____

Notes: _____

_____

Name: _____

Website Address: _____

ID/Username: _____

Password: _____

Notes: _____

_____

Name: _____

Website Address: _____

ID/Username: _____

Password: _____

Notes: _____

_____

Name: _____

Website Address: _____

ID/Username: _____

Password: _____

Notes: _____

_____

Name: _____

Website Address: _____

ID/Username: _____

Password: _____

Notes: _____

_____

Name: _____

Website Address: _____

ID/Username: _____

Password: _____

Notes: _____

_____

Name: _____

Website Address: _____

ID/Username: _____

Password: _____

Notes: _____

_____

Name: _____

Website Address: _____

ID/Username: _____

Password: _____

Notes: _____

_____

Name: _____

Website Address: _____

ID/Username: _____

Password: _____

Notes: _____

_____

Name: _____

Website Address: _____

ID/Username: _____

Password: _____

Notes: _____

_____

Name: _____

Website Address: _____

ID/Username: _____

Password: _____

Notes: _____

_____

Name: _____

Website Address: _____

ID/Username: _____

Password: _____

Notes: _____

_____

Name: _____

Website Address: _____

ID/Username: _____

Password: _____

Notes: _____

_____

Name: _____

Website Address: _____

ID/Username: _____

Password: _____

Notes: _____

_____

Name: _____

Website Address: _____

ID/Username: _____

Password: _____

Notes: _____

_____

Name: _____

Website Address: _____

ID/Username: _____

Password: _____

Notes: _____

_____

Name: _____

Website Address: _____

ID/Username: _____

Password: _____

Notes: _____

_____

Name: _____

Website Address: _____

ID/Username: _____

Password: _____

Notes: _____

_____

Name: _____

Website Address: _____

ID/Username: _____

Password: _____

Notes: _____

_____

Name: _____

Website Address: _____

ID/Username: _____

Password: _____

Notes: _____

_____

Name: _____

Website Address: _____

ID/Username: _____

Password: _____

Notes: _____

_____

Name: _____

Website Address: _____

ID/Username: _____

Password: _____

Notes: _____

_____

Name: _____

Website Address: _____

ID/Username: _____

Password: _____

Notes: _____

_____

Name: _____

Website Address: _____

ID/Username: _____

Password: _____

Notes: _____

_____

Name: _____

Website Address: _____

ID/Username: _____

Password: _____

Notes: _____

_____

Name: _____

Website Address: _____

ID/Username: _____

Password: _____

Notes: _____

_____

Name: _____

Website Address: _____

ID/Username: _____

Password: _____

Notes: _____

_____

Name: _____

Website Address: _____

ID/Username: _____

Password: _____

Notes: _____

_____

Name: _____

Website Address: _____

ID/Username: _____

Password: _____

Notes: _____

_____

Name: _____

Website Address: _____

ID/Username: _____

Password: _____

Notes: _____

_____

Name: _____

Website Address: _____

ID/Username: _____

Password: _____

Notes: _____

_____

Name: _____

Website Address: _____

ID/Username: _____

Password: _____

Notes: _____

_____

Name: _____

Website Address: _____

ID/Username: _____

Password: _____

Notes: _____

_____

Name: _____

Website Address: _____

ID/Username: _____

Password: _____

Notes: _____

_____

Name: _____

Website Address: _____

ID/Username: _____

Password: _____

Notes: _____

_____

Name: _____

Website Address: _____

ID/Username: _____

Password: _____

Notes: _____

_____

Name: _____

Website Address: _____

ID/Username: _____

Password: _____

Notes: _____

_____

Name: _____

Website Address: _____

ID/Username: _____

Password: _____

Notes: _____

_____

Name: _____

Website Address: _____

ID/Username: _____

Password: _____

Notes: _____

_____

Name: _____

Website Address: _____

ID/Username: _____

Password: _____

Notes: _____

_____

Name: _____

Website Address: _____

ID/Username: _____

Password: _____

Notes: _____

_____

Name: _____

Website Address: _____

ID/Username: _____

Password: _____

Notes: _____

_____

Name: _____

Website Address: _____

ID/Username: _____

Password: _____

Notes: _____

_____

Name: _____

Website Address: _____

ID/Username: _____

Password: _____

Notes: _____

_____

Name: _____

Website Address: _____

ID/Username: _____

Password: _____

Notes: _____

_____

Name: _____

Website Address: _____

ID/Username: _____

Password: _____

Notes: _____

_____

Name: _____

Website Address: _____

ID/Username: _____

Password: _____

Notes: _____

_____

Name: _____

Website Address: _____

ID/Username: _____

Password: _____

Notes: _____

_____

Name: _____

Website Address: _____

ID/Username: _____

Password: _____

Notes: _____

_____

Name: _____

Website Address: _____

ID/Username: _____

Password: _____

Notes: _____

_____

Name: _____

Website Address: _____

ID/Username: _____

Password: _____

Notes: _____

_____

Name: _____

Website Address: _____

ID/Username: _____

Password: _____

Notes: _____

_____

Name: _____

Website Address: _____

ID/Username: _____

Password: _____

Notes: _____

_____

Name: _____

Website Address: _____

ID/Username: _____

Password: _____

Notes: _____

_____

Name: _____

Website Address: _____

ID/Username: _____

Password: _____

Notes: _____

_____

Name: _____

Website Address: _____

ID/Username: _____

Password: _____

Notes: _____

_____

Name: _____

Website Address: _____

ID/Username: _____

Password: _____

Notes: _____

_____

Name: _____

Website Address: _____

ID/Username: _____

Password: _____

Notes: _____

_____

Name: _____

Website Address: _____

ID/Username: _____

Password: _____

Notes: _____

_____

Name: _____

Website Address: _____

ID/Username: _____

Password: _____

Notes: _____

_____

Name: _____

Website Address: _____

ID/Username: _____

Password: _____

Notes: _____

_____

Name: _____

Website Address: _____

ID/Username: _____

Password: _____

Notes: _____

_____

Name: _____

Website Address: _____

ID/Username: _____

Password: _____

Notes: _____

_____

Name: _____

Website Address: _____

ID/Username: _____

Password: _____

Notes: _____

_____

Name: _____

Website Address: _____

ID/Username: _____

Password: _____

Notes: _____

_____

Name: _____

Website Address: _____

ID/Username: _____

Password: _____

Notes: _____

_____

Name: _____

Website Address: _____

ID/Username: _____

Password: _____

Notes: _____

_____

Name: _____

Website Address: _____

ID/Username: _____

Password: _____

Notes: _____

_____

Name: _____

Website Address: _____

ID/Username: _____

Password: _____

Notes: _____

_____

Name: _____

Website Address: _____

ID/Username: _____

Password: _____

Notes: _____

_____

Name: _____

Website Address: _____

ID/Username: _____

Password: _____

Notes: _____

_____

Name: _____

Website Address: _____

ID/Username: _____

Password: _____

Notes: _____

_____

Name: _____

Website Address: _____

ID/Username: _____

Password: _____

Notes: _____

_____

Name: _____

Website Address: _____

ID/Username: _____

Password: _____

Notes: _____

_____

Name: _____

Website Address: _____

ID/Username: _____

Password: _____

Notes: _____

_____

Name: _____

Website Address: _____

ID/Username: _____

Password: _____

Notes: _____

_____

Name: _____

Website Address: _____

ID/Username: _____

Password: _____

Notes: _____

_____

Name: _____

Website Address: _____

ID/Username: _____

Password: _____

Notes: _____

_____

Name: _____

Website Address: _____

ID/Username: _____

Password: _____

Notes: _____

_____

Name: _____

Website Address: _____

ID/Username: _____

Password: _____

Notes: _____

_____

Name: _____

Website Address: _____

ID/Username: _____

Password: _____

Notes: _____

_____

Name: _____

Website Address: _____

ID/Username: _____

Password: _____

Notes: _____

_____

Name: _____

Website Address: _____

ID/Username: _____

Password: _____

Notes: _____

_____

Name: _____

Website Address: _____

ID/Username: _____

Password: _____

Notes: _____

_____

Name: _____

Website Address: _____

ID/Username: _____

Password: _____

Notes: _____

_____

Name: _____

Website Address: _____

ID/Username: _____

Password: _____

Notes: _____

_____

Name: _____

Website Address: _____

ID/Username: _____

Password: _____

Notes: _____

_____

Name: _____

Website Address: _____

ID/Username: _____

Password: _____

Notes: _____

_____

Name: _____

Website Address: _____

ID/Username: _____

Password: _____

Notes: _____

_____

Name: _____

Website Address: _____

ID/Username: _____

Password: _____

Notes: _____

_____

Name: _____

Website Address: _____

ID/Username: _____

Password: _____

Notes: _____

_____

Name: _____

Website Address: _____

ID/Username: _____

Password: _____

Notes: _____

_____

Name: _____

Website Address: _____

ID/Username: _____

Password: _____

Notes: _____

_____

Name: _____

Website Address: _____

ID/Username: _____

Password: _____

Notes: _____

_____

www.ingramcontent.com/pod-product-compliance
Lightning Source LLC
Chambersburg PA
CBHW081335090426
42737CB00017B/3151